WE WOULDN'T BE THE TEAM THAT WE ARE WITHOUT YOU

Thank You

This Journal — Notebook belongs to:

_____

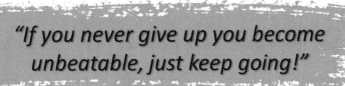

"If you never give up you become unbeatable, just keep going!"

"Thank You for All Your Hard Work and Dedication BEST TEAM EVER!"

Date: /   /

- Eat junk food

- Get ready

- Where pj's

- Pick movie

- Get Lights

THINGS TO BE GRATEFUL FOR TODAY

"Let your dreams be as big as your desire to succeed"

Date: ___ / ___ / ___

_____

_____

_____

_____

_____

_____

_____

_____

_____

_____

_____

_____

_____

_____

_____

_____

_____

_____

THINGS TO BE GRATEFUL FOR TODAY

"Never downgrade your dreams, reach for the stars and believe in your self power"

Date: /   /

_____

_____

_____

_____

_____

_____

_____

_____

_____

_____

_____

_____

_____

_____

_____

_____

THINGS TO BE GRATEFUL FOR TODAY

Date: /   /

THINGS TO BE GRATEFUL FOR TODAY

Date: /   /

_____

_____

_____

_____

_____

_____

_____

_____

_____

_____

_____

_____

_____

_____

_____

_____

_____

THINGS TO BE GRATEFUL FOR TODAY

Date: /   /

THINGS TO BE GRATEFUL FOR TODAY

> *"Wherever you go, go with all your heart."*
> *- Confucius*

Date: _____ / _____ / _____

_____
_____
_____
_____
_____
_____
_____
_____
_____
_____
_____
_____
_____
_____
_____
_____
_____
_____

THINGS TO BE GRATEFUL FOR TODAY

"Never Ever Give Up"

Date: /   /

THINGS TO BE GRATEFUL FOR TODAY

> *"Your dreams and your goals are the seeds of your own success"*

Date: /   /

_____
_____
_____
_____
_____
_____
_____
_____
_____
_____
_____
_____
_____
_____
_____
_____
_____
_____
_____
_____
_____
_____

THINGS TO BE GRATEFUL FOR TODAY

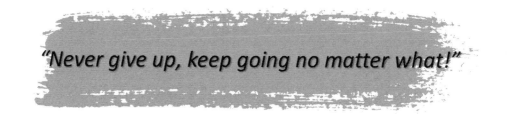

"Never give up, keep going no matter what!"

Date: / /

THINGS TO BE GRATEFUL FOR TODAY

> *"Start where you are and take chances"*

Date: /   /

_____

_____

_____

_____

_____

_____

_____

_____

_____

_____

_____

_____

_____

_____

_____

_____

_____

THINGS TO BE GRATEFUL FOR TODAY

"keep taking chances - make life a beautiful experience and never give up"

Date: /   /

THINGS TO BE GRATEFUL FOR TODAY

"Life isn't about finding yourself. Life is about creating yourself." - George Bernard Shaw

Date: /   /

_____

_____

_____

_____

_____

_____

_____

_____

_____

_____

_____

_____

_____

_____

_____

_____

THINGS TO BE GRATEFUL FOR TODAY

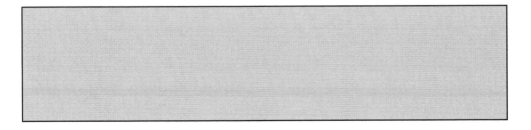

> *"Change your life today. Don't gamble on the future, act now, without delay."* — *Simone de Beauvoir*

Date: /   /

_____

_____

_____

_____

_____

_____

_____

_____

_____

_____

_____

_____

_____

_____

_____

THINGS TO BE GRATEFUL FOR TODAY

Date: /   /

_____

_____

_____

_____

_____

_____

_____

_____

_____

_____

_____

_____

_____

_____

_____

_____

_____

_____

THINGS TO BE GRATEFUL FOR TODAY

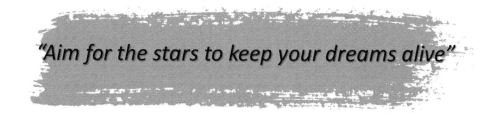

"Aim for the stars to keep your dreams alive"

Date: /   /

THINGS TO BE GRATEFUL FOR TODAY

"When life gives you lemons, add a little gin and tonic"

Date: /   /

THINGS TO BE GRATEFUL FOR TODAY

> *"There are no limits to what you can achieve
> if you believe in your dreams"*

Date: /   /

THINGS TO BE GRATEFUL FOR TODAY

"When you feel you are defeated, just remember, you have the power to move on, it is all in your mind"

Date: /   /

THINGS TO BE GRATEFUL FOR TODAY

> *"Don't just dream your dreams, make them happen!"*

Date: / /

_____

_____

_____

_____

_____

_____

_____

_____

_____

_____

_____

_____

_____

_____

_____

_____

THINGS TO BE GRATEFUL FOR TODAY

"Opportunity comes to those who never give up"

Date: /   /

THINGS TO BE GRATEFUL FOR TODAY

"You are the creator of your own opportunities"

Date: /   /

_____

_____

_____

_____

_____

_____

_____

_____

_____

_____

_____

_____

_____

_____

_____

_____

_____

THINGS TO BE GRATEFUL FOR TODAY

> *"Always aim for bigger goals, they have the power to keep you motivated"*

Date: /   /

_____

_____

_____

_____

_____

_____

_____

_____

_____

_____

_____

_____

_____

_____

_____

_____

_____

THINGS TO BE GRATEFUL FOR TODAY

"Success is not a place or a destination, it is a way of thinking while always having a new goal in mind"

Date: /   /

THINGS TO BE GRATEFUL FOR TODAY

Date: /   /

THINGS TO BE GRATEFUL FOR TODAY

> *"Change the world one dream at a time, believe in your dreams"*

Date: /   /

_____

_____

_____

_____

_____

_____

_____

_____

_____

_____

_____

_____

_____

_____

_____

_____

_____

_____

THINGS TO BE GRATEFUL FOR TODAY

"Never loose confidence in your dreams, there will be obstacles and defeats, but you will always win if you persist"

Date: /   /

_____
_____
_____
_____
_____
_____
_____
_____
_____
_____
_____
_____
_____
_____
_____
_____
_____
_____
_____

THINGS TO BE GRATEFUL FOR TODAY

Date: / /

_____

_____

_____

_____

_____

_____

_____

_____

_____

_____

_____

_____

_____

_____

_____

_____

_____

THINGS TO BE GRATEFUL FOR TODAY

"Dreams are the energy that power your life"

Date: /   /

_____

_____

_____

_____

_____

_____

_____

_____

_____

_____

_____

_____

_____

_____

_____

_____

_____

_____

THINGS TO BE GRATEFUL FOR TODAY

Date: /   /

THINGS TO BE GRATEFUL FOR TODAY

"Always dream big and follow your heart"

Date: /   /

THINGS TO BE GRATEFUL FOR TODAY

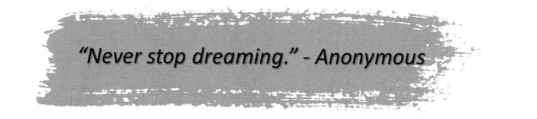

"Never stop dreaming." - Anonymous

Date: ___ / ___ / ___

THINGS TO BE GRATEFUL FOR TODAY

> *"Everything you dream is possible as long as you believe in yourself"*

Date: /   /

_____

_____

_____

_____

_____

_____

_____

_____

_____

_____

_____

_____

_____

_____

_____

_____

_____

THINGS TO BE GRATEFUL FOR TODAY

Date: /   /

THINGS TO BE GRATEFUL FOR TODAY

"A successful person is someone that understands temporary defeat as a learning process, never give up!"

Date: /   /

THINGS TO BE GRATEFUL FOR TODAY

Date: /   /

_____

_____

_____

_____

_____

_____

_____

_____

_____

_____

_____

_____

_____

_____

_____

_____

_____

THINGS TO BE GRATEFUL FOR TODAY

"Dreams are the foundation to our imagination and success"

Date: /   /

_____

_____

_____

_____

_____

_____

_____

_____

_____

_____

_____

_____

_____

_____

_____

_____

_____

THINGS TO BE GRATEFUL FOR TODAY

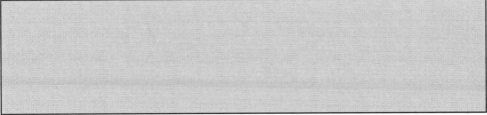

Date: /   /

THINGS TO BE GRATEFUL FOR TODAY

> *"Doing what you believe in, and going after your dreams will only result in success."* - Anonymous

Date: /   /

THINGS TO BE GRATEFUL FOR TODAY

"The right time to start something new is now"

Date: /   /

_____
_____
_____
_____
_____
_____
_____
_____
_____
_____
_____
_____
_____
_____
_____
_____
_____

THINGS TO BE GRATEFUL FOR TODAY

"Be brave, fight for what you believe in and make your dreams a reality." - Anonymous

Date: /   /

THINGS TO BE GRATEFUL FOR TODAY

Date: /   /

THINGS TO BE GRATEFUL FOR TODAY

"Let your dreams be bigger than your fears and your actions louder than your words." - Anonymous

Date: /   /
_____

_____

_____

_____

_____

_____

_____

_____

_____

_____

_____

_____

_____

_____

_____

_____

_____

_____

THINGS TO BE GRATEFUL FOR TODAY

"Always keep moving forward to keep your balance, if you stop dreaming you will fall"

Date: /   /

THINGS TO BE GRATEFUL FOR TODAY

Date: /   /

_____

_____

_____

_____

_____

_____

_____

_____

_____

_____

_____

_____

_____

_____

_____

_____

_____

_____

_____

THINGS TO BE GRATEFUL FOR TODAY

Date: /   /

THINGS TO BE GRATEFUL FOR TODAY

> *"You are never to old to set new goals and achieve them, keep on dreaming!"*

Date: /   /

_____

_____

_____

_____

_____

_____

_____

_____

_____

_____

_____

_____

_____

_____

_____

_____

_____

THINGS TO BE GRATEFUL FOR TODAY

> *"If you have big dreams you will always have big reasons to wake up every day"*

Date: /   /

_____

_____

_____

_____

_____

_____

_____

_____

_____

_____

_____

_____

_____

_____

_____

THINGS TO BE GRATEFUL FOR TODAY

"Difficulties are nothing more than opportunities in disguise, keep on trying and you will succeed"

Date: /   /

THINGS TO BE GRATEFUL FOR TODAY

Date: /   /

THINGS TO BE GRATEFUL FOR TODAY

"Always have a powerful reason to wake up every new morning, set goals and follow your dreams"

Date: /   /

THINGS TO BE GRATEFUL FOR TODAY

"Use failure as a motivation tool not as a sign of defeat"

Date: /   /

THINGS TO BE GRATEFUL FOR TODAY

*"Never let your dreams die for fear of failure,
defeat is just temporary; your dreams are your power"*

Date: /   /

THINGS TO BE GRATEFUL FOR TODAY

"A failure is a lesson, not a loss. It is a temporary and sometimes necessary detour, not a dead end"

Date: /   /

THINGS TO BE GRATEFUL FOR TODAY

"Have faith in the future but above all in yourself"

Date: /   /

_____

_____

_____

_____

_____

_____

_____

_____

_____

_____

_____

_____

_____

_____

_____

_____

_____

_____

THINGS TO BE GRATEFUL FOR TODAY

> *"Those who live in the past limit their future"*
> *- Anonymous*

Date: /   /

_____

_____

_____

_____

_____

_____

_____

_____

_____

_____

_____

_____

_____

_____

_____

_____

_____

THINGS TO BE GRATEFUL FOR TODAY

Date: /   /

_____

_____

_____

_____

_____

_____

_____

_____

_____

_____

_____

_____

_____

_____

_____

_____

_____

THINGS TO BE GRATEFUL FOR TODAY

"Never let your doubt blind your goals, for your future lies in your ability, not your failure" — Anonymous

Date: / /

_____

_____

_____

_____

_____

_____

_____

_____

_____

_____

_____

_____

_____

_____

_____

_____

THINGS TO BE GRATEFUL FOR TODAY

> *"Don't go into something to test the waters,*
> *go into things to make waves"* — *Anonymous*

Date: /   /

_____

_____

_____

_____

_____

_____

_____

_____

_____

_____

_____

_____

_____

_____

_____

THINGS TO BE GRATEFUL FOR TODAY

> *"Laughter is the shock absorber that softens and minimizes the bumps of life"* — Anonymous

Date: / /

THINGS TO BE GRATEFUL FOR TODAY

"Dream – Believe – Achieve"

Date: /   /

THINGS TO BE GRATEFUL FOR TODAY

> *"Make your own destiny. Don't wait for it to come to you, life is not a rehearsal"* — Anonymous

Date: /   /

_____

_____

_____

_____

_____

_____

_____

_____

_____

_____

_____

_____

_____

_____

_____

_____

_____

THINGS TO BE GRATEFUL FOR TODAY

Date: / /

_____

_____

_____

_____

_____

_____

_____

_____

_____

_____

_____

_____

_____

_____

THINGS TO BE GRATEFUL FOR TODAY

> *"Never give up on a dream just because of the time it will take to accomplish it. The time will pass anyway."* – Anonymous

Date: /   /

THINGS TO BE GRATEFUL FOR TODAY

"I am never a failure until I begin blaming others"
- Anonymous

Date: /   /

THINGS TO BE GRATEFUL FOR TODAY

Date: /   /

THINGS TO BE GRATEFUL FOR TODAY

Date: /   /

_____

_____

_____

_____

_____

_____

_____

_____

_____

_____

_____

_____

_____

_____

_____

_____

THINGS TO BE GRATEFUL FOR TODAY

"Anything worth doing is worth doing well"
— Anonymous

Date: /   /

_____

_____

_____

_____

_____

_____

_____

_____

_____

_____

_____

_____

_____

_____

_____

_____

_____

THINGS TO BE GRATEFUL FOR TODAY

> *"It's better to have an impossible dream than no dream at all."* – Anonymous

Date: /   /

_____

_____

_____

_____

_____

_____

_____

_____

_____

_____

_____

_____

_____

_____

_____

_____

_____

THINGS TO BE GRATEFUL FOR TODAY

"Never let defeat have the last word" — Anonymous

Date: /   /

THINGS TO BE GRATEFUL FOR TODAY

Date: /   /

_____

_____

_____

_____

_____

_____

_____

_____

_____

_____

_____

_____

_____

_____

_____

_____

_____

THINGS TO BE GRATEFUL FOR TODAY

"There is no elevator to success.
You have to take the stairs" — *Anonymous*

Date: ___ / ___ / ___

THINGS TO BE GRATEFUL FOR TODAY

"Don't let yesterday's disappointments, overshadow tomorrow's achievements" — *Anonymous*

Date: /   /

_____

_____

_____

_____

_____

_____

_____

_____

_____

_____

_____

_____

_____

_____

_____

_____

_____

THINGS TO BE GRATEFUL FOR TODAY

"We are limited, not by our abilities, but by our vision"
— Anonymous

Date: /   /

_____

_____

_____

_____

_____

_____

_____

_____

_____

_____

_____

_____

_____

_____

_____

_____

_____

_____

THINGS TO BE GRATEFUL FOR TODAY

> *"Dreams don't come true. Dreams are true"*
> *— Anonymous*

Date: /   /

THINGS TO BE GRATEFUL FOR TODAY

> *"Happiness is not something you get,
> but something you do"* — Anonymous

Date: /   /

THINGS TO BE GRATEFUL FOR TODAY

Date: /   /

THINGS TO BE GRATEFUL FOR TODAY

"Try and fail, but don't fail to try" — *Anonymous*

Date: /   /

THINGS TO BE GRATEFUL FOR TODAY

"You risk more when you don't take any risks"

Date: /   /

THINGS TO BE GRATEFUL FOR TODAY

> *"A diamond is a chunk of coal that made good under pressure"* — Anonymous

Date: /   /

_____

_____

_____

_____

_____

_____

_____

_____

_____

_____

_____

_____

_____

_____

_____

_____

_____

_____

_____

THINGS TO BE GRATEFUL FOR TODAY

> *"No dreamer is ever too small; no dream is ever too big." – Anonymous*

Date: /   /

_____

_____

_____

_____

_____

_____

_____

_____

_____

_____

_____

_____

_____

_____

_____

_____

_____

THINGS TO BE GRATEFUL FOR TODAY

"All our tomorrows depend on today" — Anonymous

Date: /   /

THINGS TO BE GRATEFUL FOR TODAY

> *"Remember yesterday, dream of tomorrow,*
> *but live for today"* — Anonymous

Date: /   /

THINGS TO BE GRATEFUL FOR TODAY

"Dream is not what you see in sleep, dream is the thing which does not let you sleep" — Anonymous

Date: / /

_____

_____

_____

_____

_____

_____

_____

_____

_____

_____

_____

_____

_____

_____

_____

_____

_____

THINGS TO BE GRATEFUL FOR TODAY

"Don't be pushed by your problems.
Be led by your dreams" — *Anonymous*

Date: /   /

_____

_____

_____

_____

_____

_____

_____

_____

_____

_____

_____

_____

_____

_____

_____

_____

_____

_____

_____

THINGS TO BE GRATEFUL FOR TODAY

> *"Dreams give purpose to your life and meaning to your existence"*

Date: /   /

THINGS TO BE GRATEFUL FOR TODAY

Date: /   /

THINGS TO BE GRATEFUL FOR TODAY

"Follow your heart and your dreams will come true"
– Anonymous

Date: /   /

THINGS TO BE GRATEFUL FOR TODAY

"You create your life by following your dreams with decisive actions"

Date: /   /

THINGS TO BE GRATEFUL FOR TODAY

Date: / /

THINGS TO BE GRATEFUL FOR TODAY

"Difficult roads often lead to beautiful destinations"

Date: /   /

_____

_____

_____

_____

_____

_____

_____

_____

_____

_____

_____

_____

_____

_____

_____

_____

_____

_____

_____

THINGS TO BE GRATEFUL FOR TODAY

Date: /   /

THINGS TO BE GRATEFUL FOR TODAY

"Believe in yourself and you will be unstoppable"

Date: /   /

THINGS TO BE GRATEFUL FOR TODAY

> *"Today is another chance to get better"*

Date: /   /

_____

_____

_____

_____

_____

_____

_____

_____

_____

_____

_____

_____

_____

_____

_____

_____

THINGS TO BE GRATEFUL FOR TODAY

"To live a creative life, we must lose our fear of being wrong" - Anonymous

Date: / /

THINGS TO BE GRATEFUL FOR TODAY

Date: /   /

_____

_____

_____

_____

_____

_____

_____

_____

_____

_____

_____

_____

_____

_____

_____

_____

_____

_____

THINGS TO BE GRATEFUL FOR TODAY

> *"If you do what you always did,*
> *you will get what you always got"* - Anonymous

Date: /   /

THINGS TO BE GRATEFUL FOR TODAY

"It's not what you look at that matters, it's what you see" - Anonymous

Date: /   /

THINGS TO BE GRATEFUL FOR TODAY

> *"You are capable of amazing things"*

Date: /   /

THINGS TO BE GRATEFUL FOR TODAY

Date: /   /

_____

_____

_____

_____

_____

_____

_____

_____

_____

_____

_____

_____

_____

_____

_____

_____

_____

_____

THINGS TO BE GRATEFUL FOR TODAY

"Successful people make a habit of doing what unsuccessful people don't want to do"
— Anonymous

Date: /   /

THINGS TO BE GRATEFUL FOR TODAY

> *"To be the best you must be able to handle the worst"* - Anonymous

Date: /   /

_____

_____

_____

_____

_____

_____

_____

_____

_____

_____

_____

_____

_____

_____

_____

_____

THINGS TO BE GRATEFUL FOR TODAY

"Nothing worth having comes easy" - Anonymous

Date: /   /

THINGS TO BE GRATEFUL FOR TODAY

"Follow your dreams, they know the way"

Date: /   /

THINGS TO BE GRATEFUL FOR TODAY

"Don't Let Anyone Dull Your Sparkle"

Date: / /

THINGS TO BE GRATEFUL FOR TODAY

CREATIVE JOURNALS FACTORY

We hope you liked your journal – notebook, please let us know if you liked it by writing a review, it means a lot to us.

Thank you!

DESIGNED BY CreativePositive Press FOR:

CREATIVE JOURNALS FACTORY

FIND OTHER BEAUTIFUL JOURNALS, DIARIES AND NOTEBOOKS AT:

www.CreativeJournalsFactory.com

JOURNALS - DIARIES - NOTEBOOKS - COLORING BOOKS

Manufactured by Amazon.ca
Bolton, ON